HORSEFIELD TO PET

A handbook guide

THE ULTIMATE MANUAL FOR KEEPING A PET HORSEFIELD TORTOISE

DR MORRIS HART

Copyright© 2024 DR **MORRIS HART**

All rights reserved. No part or part of this book or publication may be reproduced, stored, or transferred in any form by electronic, mechanical, recording, or other retrieval system without written permission Of the publisher

Table of Contents

A BRIEF OVERVIEW OF HORSEFIELD TORTOISES 4

CHAPTER 1 9
    CREATING THE IDEAL ENVIRONMENT 9

CHAPTER 2 16
    SELECTING THE APPROPRIATE TORTOISE: TYPES & VARIETIES 16

CHAPTER 3 23
    GUIDELINES FOR DIET AND FEEDING 23

CHAPTER 5 30
    MANAGING AND COMMUNICATION POINTERS 30

CHAPTER 6 37
    HEALTH AND TYPICAL PROBLEMS 37

CHAPTER 7 46
    BREEDING AND REPRODUCTION INSIGHTS 46

CHAPTER 8 55
    COMMONLY ASKED QUESTIONS 55
    SUMMARY 62

A Brief Overview of Horsefield Tortoises

The horsefield tortoise, also called the Russian tortoise after the naturalist Thomas Horsfield, is a small species of tortoise native to Central Asia, specifically Afghanistan, Pakistan, Iran, and parts of China. Its scientific name is Agrionemys horsfieldii, or Testudo horsfieldii.

Phylogeny and Natural Environment
Horsefield tortoises are members of the family Testudinidae and are categorized under the genus Agrionemys. They are well known for their capacity to survive in arid and semi-arid conditions, which are marked by rocky terrain, low vegetation, and high temperatures. Grasslands, steppes, and scrublands are among their natural habitats, providing plenty of opportunities for basking and grazing.

- Physical attributes

Horsefield tortoises have a few unique physical characteristics that add to their allure and hardiness as pets. These qualities include:

Size: When fully mature, they usually reach lengths of 5 to 8 inches (12 to 20 cm), making them smaller than other species of tortoises.

Shell: The domed carapace, or shell, is typically yellowish-brown to olive-green in color. It is frequently decorated with black blotches or patterns that help the animal blend in with its natural surroundings.

Legs: They have strong, clawed limbs that are designed for digging and scrambling over rough ground.

Head and Tail: Typical of terrestrial tortoises, their short, blunt tails are accompanied by small, triangular heads with prominent scales.

- Conduct and Attitude

It's essential to comprehend Horsefield tortoises' behavior in order to give them the best care possible in captivity:

Basking is vital to the general health and well-being of reptiles because, like other reptiles, they are dependent on outside heat sources to maintain their body temperature.

Feeding Habits: They are mostly herbivorous, eating mostly vegetables and leafy greens with the occasional fruit. It is important to provide them a balanced diet high in calcium and vitamins to ensure their long life.

Activity Levels: Horsefield tortoises love to explore their surroundings and have plenty of room to walk around, but they are not very social animals and do not need the company of other tortoises to keep them company.

Hibernation: During the winter months, Horsefield tortoises hibernate in their native habitat. It is crucial to replicate this cycle of dormancy in captivity, under carefully monitored conditions, for the long-term well-being of these animals.

- Housing and Captive Care

Creating a setting that closely resembles the Horsefield tortoise's native habitat is essential to successfully maintaining one as a pet:

Setup of the Enclosure: To keep them from escaping and to keep predators away from them, a large enclosure with a tight-fitting cover is necessary. The substrate in the enclosure should be something that allows them to burrow and dig, like a soil-and-sand mixture.

Temperature and Lighting: It is essential to keep the enclosure at an appropriate temperature gradient. To ensure optimal calcium absorption and prevent metabolic bone disease, a basking spot should be provided with temperatures between 85°F and 95°F (29°C to 35°C), while cooler areas should be between 70°F and 80°F (21°C to 27°C). UVB lighting is also required.

Hydration and Humidity: Access to a shallow water dish for drinking and bathing is necessary. The enclosure should be kept at a moderate humidity level (between 50% and 60%) to avoid shell problems and dehydration.

- Health-Related Concerns and Typical Problems

In order to maintain the longevity and general health of Horsefield tortoises, proactive healthcare is essential:

Shell Health: It's important to check the shell frequently for damage or discoloration. Inadequate humidity or unfavorable substrate conditions can lead to problems like shell rot.

Respiratory Health: Preventing respiratory infections, which can be harmful to their health, can be accomplished by keeping the enclosure properly ventilated and avoiding drafts.

Diseases and Parasites: Reducing the risk of parasites and infectious diseases requires routine veterinarian examinations as well as upkeep of a clean environment.

Horsefield tortoises are interesting animals that can make rewarding pets for those who are willing to give them the specialized care they need. Pet owners can create an environment where these hardy tortoises can thrive for decades by learning about their natural behaviors, preferences for habitats, dietary requirements, and health issues. With the right care and attention to detail, owning a Horsefield tortoise can be a rewarding experience that offers insights into the wonders of the natural world and the distinctive qualities of these fascinating reptiles.

Chapter 1

Creating the Ideal Environment

A well-designed enclosure should replicate the natural environment of these tortoises while providing all the necessary elements for their comfort, nutrition, and physiological needs. This comprehensive guide will walk you through the essential steps and considerations for setting up the ideal habitat for your Horsefield tortoise. Provided properly, a habitat is essential to the health, well-being, and longevity of a Horsefield tortoise.

Comprehending the Horsefield Tortoises' Natural Environment

Horsefield tortoises are native to arid and semi-arid regions of Central Asia, where they live in grasslands, steppes, and scrublands with rocky terrain, sparse vegetation, and extreme temperature swings. Creating a suitable captive environment requires an understanding of the natural habitat of horsefield tortoises.

Climate: Horsefield tortoises have adapted to the scorching summers and chilly winters of Central Asia, including periods of hibernating throughout the winter.

Terrain: Its native habitat typically consists of rocks, dry plants, and sandy soil, and they are used to uneven terrain with opportunities for digging and burrowing.

Behavior: In the wild, Horsefield tortoises graze on a variety of grasses, weeds, and other vegetation and spend a large portion of their time basking in the sun to regulate their body temperature.

A Comprehensive Guide for Establishing the Ideal Environment

1. Size and Selection of Enclosures

The first step in building a proper environment for your Horsefield turtle is selecting the appropriate enclosure:

- Size: Your tortoise should have enough room in its habitat to allow for proper roaming, exploring, and exercising. As a general rule of thumb, each adult tortoise should have at least 10 square feet (or 1 square meter) of area.

- Material: Because glass terrariums don't allow for adequate ventilation and are hard to keep at the right humidity levels, it's best to have a big, robust enclosure made of wood, PVC, or plastic that is safe for tortoises.

2. Matrix

Selecting the appropriate substrate is essential since it affects the tortoise's capacity to burrow, dig, and maintain good hygiene:

- Substrate Types: Dusty or containing chemicals or fertilizers is not a good substrate for Horsefield tortoises. Instead, a mixture of dirt, sand, and coconut coir is ideal since it permits natural activities like digging and nesting.
- Depth: To support natural digging habits, provide a substrate layer deep enough for your tortoise to burrow comfortably—at least 6 to 8 inches (15 to 20 cm).

3. Light and Temperature

Horsefield tortoises require appropriate illumination and temperature gradient maintenance in order to be healthy and happy.

- Basking Spot: Establish a spot where people can bask that is between 85°F and 95°F (29°C and 35°C), usually beneath a heat lamp or ceramic heat emitter. Regularly check the temperature there using a thermometer.
- Cool Zone: Provide sections of the cage that are colder, between 70°F and 80°F (21°C and 27°C). This will let the tortoise to move between warmer and colder zones to control its body temperature.
- UVB Lighting: Use a UVB fluorescent tube lamp made specifically for reptiles, and replace it every six to twelve months in accordance with manufacturer recommendations. UVB lighting is essential for healthy calcium absorption and shell integrity.

4. Water and Humidity

Important components of habitat setting include keeping humidity levels acceptable and granting access to water:

- Humidity Levels: To ensure proper moisture, use a hygrometer to measure the humidity levels and spritz the cage as needed. Horsefield tortoises need moderate humidity levels, which should be between 50% and 60%.

- Water Dish: Make sure your tortoise has access to a sturdy, shallow dish of water that is big enough for it to soak in and sip from without drowning.

5. Accentuation and Beautification

Improve the natural décor and enrichment options in your tortoise's habitat:

- Rocks and Hides: To create hiding places and climbing chances, place smooth rocks, logs, and hides inside the cage. Make sure that the décor is stable and cannot fall over.
- Plants: Avoid harmful plants and make sure plants are pesticide-free. Use tortoise-safe plants, such as edible greens (e.g., dandelion, plantain), to provide natural grazing options.

6. Upkeep and Cleaning

A good habitat for tortoises requires routine cleaning and upkeep:

- Spot Cleaning: To keep things clean, remove leftover food and excrement every day.

- Substrate Replacement: Depending on its cleanliness and condition, replace the substrate every three to six months.
- Disinfection: To stop the growth of bacteria, routinely clean and disinfect water dishes and décor.

7. Observation and Modifications

Regularly check on the behavior, well-being, and habitat circumstances of your tortoise:

- Behavioral Observation: Keep an eye out for indications of disease, stress, or unusual conduct.
- Temperature and Humidity Checks: Every day, check the conditions of your habitat using a thermometer and a hygrometer.
- Veterinary Care: To make sure your tortoise stays healthy, schedule routine examinations with a veterinarian that specializes in reptiles.

With careful planning, close attention to detail, and a dedication to providing a safe and stimulating environment, you can create the ideal habitat for a Horsefield tortoise and guarantee that it thrives in captivity. Keep in mind that every tortoise is different, so observing its behavior and making necessary adjustments will help maintain its health and happiness for years to come. With the right care and attention to detail, owning a Horsefield tortoise can be a rewarding experience, allowing you to observe and appreciate the natural behaviors of these fascinating reptiles firsthand.

Chapter 2

Selecting the Appropriate Tortoise: Types & Varieties

Selecting the proper species and variety of tortoise is an important choice for potential owners because different species have different care needs, habits, and traits. This extensive guide will go over many factors to take into account when choosing a tortoise, with a special emphasis on Horsefield tortoises (Agrionemys horsfieldii) and other popular species that are frequently kept as pets.

Recognizing the Diversity of Tortoise Species

In order to ensure proper care and husbandry, it is important to research and understand the unique traits of each species when choosing a tortoise as a pet. Tortoises are members of the Testudinidae family, which is made up of numerous genera and species that are distributed across different continents. Each species has adapted to specific habitats and environmental conditions, influencing their dietary preferences, behavior, size, and lifespan.

Popular Types and Varieties of Tortoises

1. The Agrionemys horsfieldii, or horsefield tortoise

Origin and Environment:

- Native Range: Central Asia, encompassing portions of China, Afghanistan, Pakistan, and Iran.
- The habitat consists of semi-arid scrublands, steppes, and grasslands with moderate temperatures and dry weather.

Physical attributes:

- Size: Relatively little; when completely grown, it can reach lengths of 5 to 8 inches (12 to 20 cm).
- Shell: Usually olive-green to yellowish-brown with dark specks or patterns, domed.
- Activity: Known for sunbathing and grazing on a range of grasses and flora, this species is diurnally active during the day.

Taking Care of Things:

- **Temperature:** Needs a warm place to bask that is between 85°F and 95°F (29°C and 35°C), and a colder place that is between 70°F and 80°F (21°C and 27°C).
- **UVB Lighting:** Crucial to overall health and appropriate calcium absorption.
- **Diet:** Mostly herbivorous, including vegetables, fruits, and leafy greens.

2. The Testudo graeca, or Greek Tortoise

Origin and Environment:

- **Native Range:** North Africa, sections of the Middle East, and Southern Europe.
- **Habitat:** rocky hillsides, grasslands, and scrublands in the Mediterranean region; dry, warm weather.

Physical attributes:

- **Dimensions:** Usually 6 to 12 inches (15 to 30 cm) in length, small to medium in size.

- Shell: Dome-shaped, varying from yellowish-brown to dark brown in hue and pattern.
- Diurnal, terrestrial behavior; burrowing and sheltering in foliage are common.

Taking Care of Things:

- Temperature: With a basking spot and cooler parts, this tortoise has similar temperature requirements to Horsefield tortoises.
- Eats a variety of greens, weeds, and occasionally flowers; it is a herbivorous diet.

3. The Centrochelys sulcata tortoise

Origin and Environment:

- Native Range: Sub-Saharan Africa, especially the savannah and Sahara Desert areas.
- Habitat: Hot, dry conditions with little vegetation in semi-arid and dry regions.

Physical attributes:

- Size: Big and strong, with a maximum weight of 100 pounds (45 kg) and a reach of more than 30 inches (76 cm).
- Shell: Scutes have deep grooves called sulci, and the shell is broad and richly patterned.
- Behavior: Diurnal, mostly terrestrial, has a reputation for digging large burrows.

Taking Care of Things:

- Habitat Size: Because of their size and space requirements, they require a sizable outside enclosure.
- Temperature: Needs to be hot and have a place to bask that is above 100°F (38°C).
- Food: Being herbivorous, they consume a diet high in fiber, which includes leafy greens, hay, and grasses.

Considerations for Selecting a Tortoise

1. Dimensions and Area Needed

Larger species, like Sulcata tortoises, often require outdoor pens due to their size and activity levels, while smaller species, like Horsefield and Greek tortoises, may thrive in indoor enclosures;

take into consideration the adult size of the tortoise species you're interested in and make sure you have enough space to accommodate their needs.

2. Needs for the Environment

The health and well-being of the tortoise species depend on creating a habitat that closely resembles their natural habitat, so research into the species' natural habitat to understand its environmental requirements, including temperature, humidity, substrate preferences, and UVB lighting demands.

3. Nutritional Preferences

Various species of tortoises have different nutritional needs and dietary preferences. Make sure you can offer a well-balanced diet high in fiber, calcium, and vitamins for the particular species you select. For feeding guidelines and dietary recommendations, speak with a veterinarian who specializes in reptiles.

4. Duration and Devotion

Taking into account the average lifespan of the species—many tortoises can live for several decades or even over a century—you can see that owning a tortoise is an investment that will need constant attention to its care, well-being, and upkeep.

5. Concerns with Law and Ethics

Verify local laws and restrictions about tortoise ownership and importation; some species may be protected or require specific licenses; ethical factors should also be taken into account, such as sourcing responsibly and avoiding buying specimens that have been captured in the wild.

Whether you choose a larger species like the Sulcata tortoise or a smaller species like the Horsefield tortoise, providing a suitable habitat with proper temperature, lighting, substrate, and diet is essential for their health and longevity. By taking the time to create an optimal environment and meeting their unique needs, you can ensure a fulfilling and enriching experience as a tortoise owner, fostering a lifelong bond with your reptilian companion. Proper research is essential to choosing the right species of tortoise.

Chapter 3

Guidelines for Diet and Feeding

Guidelines for Feeding and Nutrition in Tortoises

Because they are herbivores, tortoises need a diet high in fiber, vitamins, and minerals to support their special physiology and digestive system. This extensive guide will cover the dietary requirements, feeding practices, and guidelines for different species of tortoises, with an emphasis on useful advice for sustaining optimal nutrition in captivity.

Recognizing the Tortoise's Natural Diet

In their natural environments, tortoises are predominantly herbivorous reptiles that eat a wide range of plant materials. Typical foods that they would eat include:

- Grass: Including several kinds of sedges and grasses.
- Leafy Greens: These include plantains, mulberry leaves, clover, and dandelion greens.
- Broadleaf weeds such as chickweed, sow thistle, and mallow are among the weeds and wildflowers.

- Fruits and Vegetables: Occasionally found fruits like melons and berries, as well as vegetables like carrots and squash.
- Replicating this varied diet in captivity is key to provide vital nutrients and enhancing general health in tortoises.

Feeding Guidelines Specific to Species

1. The Agrionemys horsfieldii, or horsefield tortoise
Nutrition:

- Greens: Provide an assortment of leafy greens, including endive, mustard, collard, and dandelion greens.
- Weeds: Add edible weeds such as sow thistle, clover, and plantain.
- Vegetables: Offer veggies including bell peppers, green beans, carrots, and squash.
- Fruits: As occasional treats, provide fruits like melons, cherries, and apples without seeds.
- Calcium: To make sure you're getting enough calcium, dust fruits and vegetables with powdered calcium.

Feeding Pattern:

- Adults: Feed adult Horsefield tortoises every day with a variety of veggies, fruits, and greens.
- Juveniles: In order to promote growth and development, juveniles may need to be fed more frequently—up to twice a day.

2. The Testudo graeca, or Greek Tortoise

Nutrition:

- Greens: Provide a range of leafy, dark greens, including Swiss chard, kale, and romaine lettuce.
- Weeds: Include edible weeds like chickweed, plantain, and dandelion greens.
- Provide veggies such as bell peppers, cucumbers, and zucchini.
- Fruits: Occasionally serve fruits, such as berries and tiny portions of apple or pear.
- Calcium: To make sure your vegetables and greens are getting enough calcium, sprinkle some calcium powder on them.

Feeding Pattern:

- Adults: Provide a daily meal of greens, veggies, and occasionally fruits to adult Greek tortoises.
- Juveniles: Like Horsefield tortoises, juveniles may need more frequent feedings to support their growth.

3. The Centrochelys sulcata tortoise

Nutrition:

- Grass: Plant grasses like Timothy hay, orchard grass, and Bermuda grass.
- Hay: Provide hay as a basic food source to help them eat like they would in arid climates.
- Leafy Greens: Add a range of deep-colored leafy greens, like kale, collard greens, and turnip greens.
- Snacky Vegetables: Serve sporadic veggies such sweet potatoes, squash, and carrots.
- Fruits: Because fruits contain a lot of sugar, use them sparingly. Instead, serve products like berries and cactus fruits.
- Calcium: Make sure you're getting enough calcium by taking supplements and eating foods high in calcium.

Feeding Pattern:

- Adults: Provide a daily meal of grasses, hay, and leafy greens to adult Sulcata tortoises.
- Juveniles: High-fiber foods should be fed more frequently to encourage a child's quick growth.

Feeding Techniques and Advice

1. Diversity Is Essential

Provide a range of foods to make sure your tortoise eats a well-balanced diet. Switch up your greens, veggies, and sometimes fruits to add some nutritional diversity and avoid nutritional deficits.

2. Steer clear of foods high in fat and protein.

Avoid fatty foods and dairy products, as these might cause digestive problems. Tortoises have low protein requirements and cannot effectively digest high-protein diets like meat, insects, or commercial dog/cat food.

3. Vitamin and Calcium Supplements

To help your tortoise avoid metabolic bone disease, add extra vitamin D3 to its diet (use calcium powder), and consider giving it an occasional multivitamin supplement designed specifically for reptiles.

4. Hydration and Water

For drinking and soaking, provide a shallow water dish that is routinely cleaned and refilled with new water to prevent dehydration. Misting the dish occasionally will also help certain tortoises drink more easily by increasing humidity.

5. Track Eating Patterns and Well-being

See a reptile veterinarian if you observe any changes in appetite, weight loss, or symptoms of nutritional inadequacies. Keep an eye on your tortoise's feeding habits and modify its diet based on hunger, growth, and general health.

Hibernation and Seasonal Variations

If you live in an area where there are various seasons, then you should modify your tortoise's diet as well. In the warmer months, add more fresh greens and vegetables. When the weather cools off, you should progressively cut back on feeding and, if your species permits it, get ready for hibernation.

For the health and well-being of tortoises, it is imperative to maintain a diet that is both balanced and nutrient-rich. By offering a variety of greens, vegetables, occasionally fruits, and suitable supplements, you can guarantee that your tortoise gets the nutrients it needs to thrive in captivity. Knowing the dietary needs and feeding habits specific to your species will help you design a feeding schedule that supports growth, vitality, and longevity for your companion tortoise. Quality and diversity in diet should always take precedence when it comes to promoting a healthy and happy life for your tortoise.

Chapter 5

Managing and Communication Pointers

Although tortoises are not usually social or affectionate like some other pets, appropriate handling techniques and respectful interaction can help minimize stress and ensure a positive experience for both the tortoise and the keeper. This comprehensive guide will explore various aspects of handling and interacting with tortoises, with a focus on safety, welfare, and fostering a bond of trust with your tortoise companion. How to handle and interact with tortoises?

Recognizing the Behavior and Features of Tortoises

Terrestrial reptiles called tortoises are distinguished by their sluggish movements, protective shells, and unusual adaptations:

- Shell: The shell is a structure of bone covered in keratinous scutes that protects the organism from predators and environmental dangers.

- Legs: Large, elephant-like limbs with claws designed for climbing, digging, and holding onto uneven surfaces are characteristic of tortoises.
- Head and Neck: The neck can retract into the shell for protection, and the head is small with a beak-like mouth that is adapted for feeding on vegetation.

In their native environment, tortoises engage in activities like eating vegetation, basking in the sun to control body temperature, and hiding inside their shells when they feel threatened or anxious.

Techniques for Managing Tortoises

To guarantee safe and stress-free handling, handle tortoises with caution and respect for their unique physiology and behavior. Here are some tips to follow:

1. Proceed Calmly and Slowly

Avoid rapid Movements: To prevent frightening your tortoise, approach it quietly and gently. Tortoises are sensitive to vibrations and rapid movements.

2. Give the tortoise the right support

Shell Support: To prevent harm, never grip or lift a tortoise by its shell alone. Instead, use both hands to support the tortoise's body evenly.

3. Lift Securely and Gently

Underbelly Support: Place one hand under the tortoise's belly and the other hand under its shell or on its sides. Lift gently and securely, ensuring the tortoise feels supported and stable.

4. Avoid Excessive Handling

Minimal Handling: Tortoises are not social animals and may become stressed with excessive handling. Limit handling sessions to necessary activities such as health checks or habitat maintenance.

5. Respect Signs of Stress

Withdrawal into Shell: If a tortoise withdraws into its shell or exhibits retracted limbs, it may be stressed or uncomfortable. Respect these signs and allow the tortoise to retreat if needed.

Interacting with Your Tortoise

While tortoises may not seek out human interaction like certain pets, you may still engage with them in ways that support their well-being and enrichment:

1. Observation and Bonding

Observation: Spend time monitoring your turtle in its habitat to understand its behaviors, preferences, and routines.

Bonding: While tortoises may not bond in the same manner as mammals, they can recognize familiar sounds and habits, gradually becoming acclimated to your presence.

2. Enrichment Activities

Exploration: Provide opportunities for your tortoise to explore its environment safely. Allow it to roam in a secure outdoor pen or monitored indoor space.

Foraging: Hide food items throughout the enclosure to encourage natural foraging habits. This encourages mental and physical activity.

3. Grooming and Health Checks

Shell Inspection: Regularly inspect your tortoise's shell for any signs of damage, discoloration, or abnormalities.

Foot Care: Check the tortoise's feet and claws for signs of overgrowth or injury. Trim nails gently if necessary, using suitable tools and techniques.

4. Interaction with the Environment

Sunshine and Basking: To support natural activities and promote general health, make sure your tortoise has access to UVB illumination and a basking location that is at a comfortable temperature.

Outside Time: Provide shade and a protective enclosure for the tortoise, and supervise outdoor excursions to guarantee its safety and protection from predators.

Typical Errors to Steer Clear of

1. Excessive manipulation

Stress: Overhandling can cause stress in tortoises, which can result in withdrawal, appetite loss, and even health problems.

2. Improper Techniques of Handling

Damage to the shell: Inadequate handling methods, such as lifting just the shell, might result in harm to the shell.

3. Insufficient Environmental Improvement

Boredom: Your turtle may become bored and lose mental stimulation if their surroundings aren't sufficiently stimulating.

4. Disregarding Health Exams

Health Issues: Undiagnosed health disorders or issues may arise from skipping routine health examinations and monitoring.

Establishing Positive Interaction and Trust

Even though tortoises aren't as affectionate as other animals, you may still create a good relationship and earn their trust by treating them with respect and consistency:

1. Equitable

Routine: Establish a consistent feeding schedule, habitat management routine, and handling technique. Predictability can lessen stress for your tortoise.

2. Observation and Patience

Understanding: Recognize indicators of comfort and discomfort in your tortoise by being patient and watching its behaviors and responses.

3. Honor Delimitations

Respect the need for calm areas and personal space that your tortoise needs in its natural habitat.

4. Encouragement

Rewards: To help associate handling and interaction with good experiences, use positive reinforcement tactics like giving favorite foods or soft stroking.

With proper handling techniques, respecting their boundaries, and offering enriching interactions, you can build a trusting relationship and ensure a positive experience for both you and your tortoise companion. Keep in mind that every tortoise is different, so pay attention to their preferences and modify your interactions accordingly to promote a happy and healthy life for your tortoise in captivity. Taking care of tortoises, especially Horsefield tortoises, requires thoughtful handling and interaction that prioritizes their natural behaviors, physical needs, and general well-being.

Chapter 6

Health and Typical Problems

Well-being and Typical Problems in Tortoises

Keeping tortoises healthy, especially species such as the Horsefield tortoise (Agrionemys horsfieldii), means being vigilant about giving the right care, keeping an eye out for symptoms, and acting quickly when something goes wrong. This extensive chapter will go over important topics related to tortoise health, such as common ailments, preventive care, and what to do in the event that a health issue arises.

Comprehending the Health of Tortoises

Understanding tortoises' natural behaviors and physiological needs is crucial for maintaining their well-being in captivity. Tortoises are resilient reptiles known for their longevity and adaptability, but they are susceptible to various health issues, influenced by factors such as habitat conditions, diet, environmental stressors, and genetics.

Features of the Body and Vital Signs

Shell: Consisting of bony plates coated in keratinous scutes, the shell provides protection. Check the shell frequently for damage, abnormalities, or shell rot.

Eyes: Clear, bright eyes are indicative of excellent health; discharge, puffiness, or cloudiness around the eyes might be signs of illness or trauma.

Skin: Smooth skin free of lesions or aberrant pigmentation is a sign of health. Skin disorders can be a sign of more serious conditions.

Breathing: Consistent breathing without wheezing or other audible noises is normal. Difficult breathing could be a sign of respiratory issues.

Activity Level: Diurnal (active during the day), tortoises should move normally and react to stimuli as expected.

Weight maintenance: Keeping an eye on your weight on a regular basis will help you check your general health and spot any changes that could point to a disease or dietary inadequacies.

Typical Health Problems in Tortoises

1. Start with respiratory infections
   - Lethargy, open-mouth breathing, nasal discharge, and wheezing are the symptoms.
   - Causes: Poor habitat conditions (low temperatures, high humidity), stress, or bacterial/fungal diseases.
   - Treatment: Depending on the underlying cause, antibiotics may be administered. Veterinary care is crucial for the diagnosis and treatment of respiratory infections.

2. Rotting Shells
   - Symptoms include the shell scutes softening, discolouration (white or black patches), bad odor, and flaking.
   - Causes: Poor cleanliness, poor substrate, or injuries that lead to bacterial or fungal diseases.
   - therapy: Provide dry, clean substrate, clean afflicted areas with diluted betadine solution, and improve hygiene. Veterinarian intervention and antibiotic therapy may be necessary in severe cases.

3. MBD, or metabolic bone disease

- Symptoms include swelling joints, a softening or deformity of the shell, lethargy, and a reluctance to move.
- Causes include inadequate UVB lighting, an unbalanced diet, and deficiencies in calcium and vitamin D3.
- Prevention: Keep an eye on calcium and vitamin intake to prevent deficits. Provide UVB lighting and a diet high in calcium.

4. Infections with Parasites
- Symptoms include weight loss, diarrhea, lethargy, and visible parasites (worms, protozoa) in the stool.
- Causes include inadequate personal cleanliness, consuming tainted food or drink, or coming into contact with sick animals.
- Treatment: Using fecal testing to diagnose the animal and administering the proper deworming or antiparasitic medicine.

5. Inadequate Nutrient intake
- Symptoms include weakness, malformations of the shell, stunted growth, and altered appetite.
- Causes: Insufficient diet deficient in vital nutrients (fiber, calcium, and vitamin D3).

- Prevention: Make sure you get enough UVB exposure for the absorption of calcium. Offer a varied diet consisting of leafy greens, vegetables, occasionally fruits, and supplements as needed.

6. Injuries and Trauma
    - Symptoms include limb injuries, wounds, bruising, and shell fractures.
    - Causes include mishaps, falls, and runs-ins with raptors or hostile cagemates.
    - Treatment: Prompt veterinary attention to assess the situation, clean wounds, and administer the necessary medications and wound care to stop infection.

7. Egg Retention (Dystocia)
    - Symptoms include lethargy, appetite loss, incapacity to lay eggs, and abdominal swelling.
    - Causes: Inadequate conditions for nesting, insufficient calcium, or egg binding.
    - Treatment: To help improve egg laying, give calcium supplements, and take care of any underlying health issues, veterinary intervention is required.

Preventive Healthcare and Marital Behavior

1. Correct Setup of Habitat

Enclosure: Provide a roomy, safe enclosure that is suitable for the native environment of the tortoise species. It should also provide UVB illumination, a suitable substrate, and humidity levels.

Cleanliness: To stop bacterial or fungal growth and lower the risk of illnesses, keep the substrate, water dishes, and enclosure clean.
Hydration: To avoid dehydration, make sure you have access to clean, fresh water for drinking and bathing.

2. Nutrition and Dietary Balance

Provide a varied diet consisting of leafy greens, veggies, sporadic fruits, and supplements (vitamin D3, calcium) as required.

Calcium Supplementation: To avoid metabolic bone disease and promote shell health, dust fruits and vegetables with calcium powder.

Steer Clear of Toxic Plants: Because certain plants and veggies can be poisonous or cause digestive problems in tortoises, do your homework before giving them any.

3. Environmental Enrichment

Natural habits: Provide opportunities for natural habits such as basking, digging, and exploring to stimulate physical and mental wellness.

Foraging: Encourage foraging behavior by hiding food items or placing them in different locations within the enclosure.

4. Regular Health Monitoring

Observation: Keep a regular eye out for any changes in your tortoise's appearance, activity level, demeanor, or hunger.

Weight Checks: Keep a regular eye on your weight to track your growth and identify any potential health issues early.

5. Veterinary Care

Annual Check-ups: Schedule annual veterinary checks with a reptile veterinarian to assess overall health, perform fecal tests, and address any issues.

Quick Attention: If your tortoise exhibits any symptoms of disease or strange behavior, get in touch with a veterinarian right once.

Managing Medical Emergencies

1. Know What Emergency Signs Are

Symptoms may include bleeding excessively, trauma, severe respiratory distress, or abrupt behavioral changes (collapse, lethargy).

Take Quick Action: Take your tortoise to a veterinarian clinic that is prepared to handle exotic animals and seek advice from a reptile doctor right once.

2. Basic First Aid

Wound Care: Use a diluted betadine solution to clean wounds, and keep an eye out for any indications of infection.

Hydration: If the tortoise appears dehydrated, give it access to fresh water and think about giving it a dip in some shallow, lukewarm water.

3. Administration of Medication

Observe Veterinarian Instructions: Give drugs exactly as directed by your veterinarian, paying close attention to dose guidelines.

A proactive approach to husbandry, nutrition, and illness detection is necessary to maintain the health and well-being of tortoises, including the Horsefield tortoise. You can create a safe and loving environment for your companion tortoise by learning about common health issues, taking preventive measures, and seeking veterinary care when necessary. Proper diet, regular habitat maintenance, and timely attention to health issues are crucial for promoting longevity and guaranteeing a happy and healthy life for your tortoise in captivity. Your tortoise's welfare should always come first, and you should always prioritize their well-being.

Chapter 7

Breeding and Reproduction Insights

Breeding and reproduction in tortoises, including species like the Horsefield tortoise (Agrionemys horsfieldii), involves understanding their natural behaviors, reproductive biology, environmental conditions necessary for successful breeding, and care considerations for hatchlings. This comprehensive guide will explore various aspects of tortoise breeding, from mating behaviors to incubation and care of hatchlings, providing insights into fostering successful reproduction in captivity.

Understanding Tortoise Reproductive Biology
Important facets of tortoise reproductive biology include: species-specific behaviors, environmental cues, seasonal fluctuations, and unique reproductive techniques displayed by tortoises.

1. Dimorphism in Sexuality
Physical Distinctions: In comparison to females, male tortoises usually have longer tails, concave plastrons (bottom shells), and bigger, more muscular rear legs.

Behavioral Differences: Males may engage in wooing activities such head bobbing, circling, and trying to mount females during the mating season.

2. Mating Patterns

Courtship: Men approach women to show their authority with head gestures and, if appropriate for their species, vocalizations.

Mating: In order for a successful mating to occur, the male must mount the female and position their cloacas so that they can copulate, which can take many hours.

3. Cycles of Reproduction

Seasonal Breeding: Seasonal reproductive cycles are exhibited by several tortoise species in response to environmental cues such temperature, humidity, and photoperiod (length of day).

Induced Ovulation: Environmental factors and successful mating can cause females to undergo induced ovulation.

4. Egg Laying and Nest Building

Nesting Behavior: When searching for a good place to build a nest, females frequently favor sandy or well-drained soil.

Laying of Eggs: Before leaving, females place their eggs in the prepared nest cavity and cover them with earth or substrate.

Prerequisites and Procedures for Breeding

1. Setup of Enclosure and Habitat
Size and Space: Provide a place for nesting or a large, safe outdoor enclosure with appropriate soil or sand for excavating.

Temperature and Lighting: To promote reproductive behaviors and the development of eggs, maintain ideal temperatures and exposure to natural sunshine.

Privacy: To lessen stress and promote natural nesting behaviors, make sure nesting sites are isolated and unaffected by outside stimuli.

2. Nutrition and Diet

Pre-breeding conditioning: Make sure adult tortoises eat a balanced diet high in calcium, vitamins, and minerals to keep them in good health.

Supplementation: To encourage the production of eggshells and general reproductive health, give calcium supplements and vitamin D3.

3. Harmony and Equivalency
Pairing: During the breeding season, introduce compatible male and female tortoises, keeping an eye on interactions to avoid stress or violence.

Species Compatibility: To preserve genetic integrity and prevent hybridization, make sure breeding couples are of the same species and subspecies.

Incubation of Eggs and Nesting

1. Nesting Patterns
Excavation: Using their front limbs and rear legs, females dig nest holes to a depth that is appropriate for laying eggs.

Laying of Eggs: Depending on the species and fertility of each individual, females lay one to multiple eggs into the nest cavity.

2. Collecting and Caring for Eggs

Examine the eggs carefully to prevent rotation or displacement from their initial orientation, as this can have an impact on the development of the embryo.

Labeling & Marking: To keep track of the incubation process and guarantee appropriate observation, mark eggs with dates or identifying codes.

3. Conditions of Incubation

Temperature and Humidity: To encourage proper embryo development, keep the incubator or natural nesting site at constant temperatures and humidity levels.

Eggs should be surrounded and supported during incubation by an appropriate incubation media, such as vermiculite or perlite.

4. The Incubation Stage

Duration: Incubation times can range from a few weeks to several months, depending on the species and the surrounding circumstances.

Monitoring: To maximize hatch rates, keep a regular eye on the incubation conditions and make necessary adjustments to the temperature and humidity.

Taking Care of Hatchlings

1. The process of hatching

Egg Pipping: As hatchlings get ready to emerge, keep an eye out for evidence of pipping, which are cracks or holes that indicate hatching activity.

Help: Refrain from getting involved unless absolutely required; help hatchlings only if they are unable to come out of the egg completely on their own.

2. Primary Care

Housing for Hatchlings: Give the hatchlings their own cage with the right substrate, temperature gradients, UVB illumination, and hiding places.

Feeding: Provide tiny portions of moistened commercial tortoise diet, finely chopped leafy greens, and calcium supplements as needed.

Hydration: To avoid dehydration, make sure hatchlings have access to shallow water dishes for drinking and bathing.

3. Expansion and Improvement

Observation: Keep a close eye on the hatchlings' growth rates, eating habits, and general health indicators.

Initial veterinary check-ups should be scheduled in order to evaluate the health of the hatchlings, administer any required immunizations, and handle any health issues.

Obstacles and Things to Think About

1. Health Hazards

Early Mortality: Developmental defects, malnutrition, and dehydration are among the health risks that hatchlings face.

Parasitic Infections: Keep an eye out for symptoms of parasitic infections, and if one is found, treat it right once under veterinary supervision.

2. Interaction and Socialization

Minimal Handling: To reduce stress and give hatchlings time to adjust to their new surroundings, limit handling to necessary care tasks.

Socialization: To develop trust over time, acclimate hatchlings to human presence gradually through quiet observation and minimal engagement.

Maintaining Records and Documentation

1. Records of Breeding

Data collection: Keep thorough records of all breeding efforts, pairings made, dates of nesting, numbers of eggs laid, and circumstances throughout incubation.

Health Records: Keep track of hatchling health evaluations, growth anniversaries, and veterinarian treatments for continued supervision and care.

2. Genetic Management

Pedigree tracking: To preserve genetic variety and stop inbreeding in captive populations, keep track of genetic lineage and parentage information.

Breeding Programs: Participate in responsible breeding programs that prioritize species conservation, genetic health, and sustainability.

The process of breeding and reproducing tortoises, like the Horsefield tortoise, requires careful planning, an understanding of natural behavior, and a dedication to providing the best care possible throughout the breeding process. By establishing appropriate habitat conditions, encouraging natural behaviors, and following appropriate husbandry practices, tortoise breeders can improve reproductive success and support conservation efforts. Responsible breeding practices involve keeping track of health, managing hatchling care, and monitoring offspring health in order to ensure the long-term viability of captive tortoise populations. In order to address specific breeding challenges and enhance the welfare of

Chapter 8

Commonly Asked Questions

Agrionemys horsfieldii, commonly called Russian tortoises, are small, hardy reptiles with distinct personalities that are popular as pets. This FAQ section answers frequently asked questions about caring for Horsefield tortoises, covering everything from habitat setup and food to behavior issues and health issues.

1. How should a Horsefield tortoise's habitat be set up?
    - Enclosure: Give adults access to a roomy enclosure that is at least 36" x 18".
    - Substrate: For burrowing, use a mixture of topsoil, sand, and coconut coir.
    - Temperature: Keep a basking spot at up to 95°F (35°C), and maintain a temperature gradient of 75-85°F (24-29°C).
    - UVB Lighting: To promote calcium absorption and shell health, provide UVB lighting for ten to twelve hours each day.
    - Humidity: To avoid respiratory problems, maintain moderate humidity levels (between 40 and 60 percent).

2. What food is OK for my Horsefield tortoise?
- Diet: Provide leafy greens (kale, dandelion greens, endive), weeds (plantains, clovers), and sometimes fruits (strawberries, apple slices).
- Calcium Supplementation: For extra calcium, sprinkle some powdered calcium over vegetables and offer a cuttlebone or calcium block.
- Water: Make sure you have everyday access to fresh water for bathing and drinking.

3. How often should I feed my Horsefield tortoise?
- Adults: Feed on a daily basis, alternating between leafy greens, veggies, and sometimes fruits.
- Feed young animals twice a day to promote healthy growth and development.

4. Do the tortoises of Horsefield hibernate?
- Natural Behavior: Yes, Horsefield tortoises are known to hibernate in the wild as a response to cooler weather and lower food supply.
- Captivity: Although not all captive tortoises hibernate, mimic natural conditions by gradually lowering

temperatures and lengthening daylight hours in advance of hibernation.

5. How should I securely handle my Horsefield tortoise?
- Approach: To prevent frightening the tortoise, approach quietly and carefully.
- Support: Don't lift the tortoise by its shell alone; instead, evenly support its body with both hands.
- Minimal Handling: To reduce stress, only handle things that are absolutely necessary.

6. What health problems are typical in Horsefield tortoises?
- Temperature or humidity imbalances can lead to respiratory infections.
- A calcium or vitamin D3 shortage is the cause of metabolic bone disease (MBD).
- Shell Rot: Caused by bacterial infections or inadequate personal hygiene.
- Internal parasites can have an impact on the health of the digestive system.

7. What can I do to keep my Horsefield tortoise healthy?

- Maintain the right humidity, temperature, and UVB lighting in the habitat.
- Nutrition: Serve a well-rounded meal rich in different greens and calcium supplements.
- Hygiene: Every day, supply new water and maintain the enclosure clean.
- Veterinary Care: See a veterinarian for reptiles on a regular basis.

8. Are Horsefield tortoises compatible with other pet tortoises?
- Horsefield tortoises get along well with other tortoises of a similar size and disposition.
- Interaction with Pets: Watch how your pet interacts with other animals to make sure it doesn't get hurt or stressed out.

9. How can I determine the gender of my Horsefield tortoise?
- Physical characteristics: In comparison to females, males usually have longer tails, concave plastrons, and thicker hind legs.
- Behavioral Variations: Males may become more combative and vocalize more during mating season.

10. Do Horsefield tortoises need any extra attention when they're breeding?
- Prepare by making sure there is enough room, a healthy nutrition, and a conducive atmosphere for mating and natural behaviors.
- Nesting: Provide a quiet place with an appropriate surface on which to build a nest and deposit eggs.
- Incubation: To ensure a successful incubation process, keep an eye on the eggs and maintain constant humidity and temperature conditions.

11. Should I take action if my horsefield tortoise refuses to eat?
- Possible causes include sickness, stress, poor nutrition, or alterations in the surroundings.
- Steps to take: Keep a close eye on things, make any required habitat adjustments, and get advice from a reptile veterinarian if appetite loss doesn't go away.

12. What is the lifespan of Horsefield tortoises?
Lifespan: With proper care, Horsefield tortoises can live 50 years or more in captivity, making them long-term companions.

13. Are Horsefield tortoises endangered?

- Conservation Status: While not officially endangered, wild populations suffer challenges from habitat loss, hunting, and climate change.
- Responsibilities: Responsible pet ownership and captive breeding programs are important components of conservation initiatives.

14. Is it okay to bring my Horsefield tortoise outdoors?
- Outside Time: It is possible to get natural sunlight and enrichment through supervised outdoor time in a safe enclosure or pen.
- Safety: Keep an eye on the surroundings and make sure you're protected from potential threats and predators.

Horsefield tortoises are fascinating reptile pets known for their resilience and unique characteristics. By understanding their specific care requirements, nutritional needs, health considerations, and natural behaviors, tortoise enthusiasts can provide a fulfilling and enriching environment for these beloved companions. Regular observation, proper diet, habitat maintenance, and veterinary care are essential in ensuring the well-being and longevity of Horsefield tortoises in captivity. For personalized advice or concerns, consult with a reptile veterinarian or experienced tortoise keeper to address specific needs and promote the health of your tortoise companion.

Summary

To sum up, taking good care of a Horsefield tortoise (Agrionemys horsfieldii) requires knowledge of its distinct features, natural behaviors, and specific needs. These tortoises are prized for their hardiness, small size, and gregarious personalities. They flourish when their husbandry practices emulate their natural habitat and guarantee their general wellbeing.

Each section of this guide has emphasized the significance of providing a safe, enriching environment where these tortoises can thrive, from establishing the ideal habitat and feeding them a balanced diet to comprehending health considerations, handling techniques, and even insights into breeding and reproduction.

For them to be in good physiological and behavioral health, their habitat must be kept at its ideal temperature gradient, have UVB lighting, and have a suitable substrate. They also need a diet high in leafy greens, vegetables, and sometimes fruits, with calcium and vitamin D3 supplements to support their growth, shell strength, and immune system.

By being aware of common health problems like respiratory infections, metabolic bone disease, and shell rot and knowing how to prevent and treat them with good hygiene, dietary changes, and prompt veterinary care, one can guarantee that tortoises stay robust and healthy for the duration of their lives.

Minimizing stress during handling and offering opportunities for enrichment activities like exploring outdoor enclosures or foraging for food items promotes the physical and mental well-being of Horsefield tortoises. Handling and interacting with these creatures should be done with patience and respect for their temperament and natural instincts.

Understanding their reproductive biology, nesting habits, and incubation requirements can help those who are interested in breeding adopt responsible breeding techniques that will produce healthy offspring and support conservation efforts.

In the end, Horsefield tortoises are rewarding pets for committed keepers who are willing to put in time, effort, and affection into their care because of their longevity and companionship. By adhering to the rules and suggestions provided in this extensive guide, tortoise enthusiasts can guarantee a happy and enriching life for their Horsefield tortoise companions, fostering a strong bond based on mutual respect, trust, and well-being.

Regardless of your level of experience, the constant education and adjustment to your tortoise's requirements will deepen your understanding of these fascinating reptile friends. By putting their health first, creating an environment that is stimulating, and valuing the individual characteristics that make each tortoise unique, you support their healthy lives and improve your own.

Printed in Great Britain
by Amazon